Journal for Grief and Healing

JOURNAL
FOR GRIEF AND HEALING

By Donnette Alfelt

FOUNTAIN PUBLISHING®
Rochester, Michigan

JOURNAL FOR GRIEF AND HEALING

Published by Fountain Publishing®
P.O. Box 80011, Rochester, Michigan 48308-0011
www.fountainpublishing.com

Cover and book design by Lisa Alfelt Eller
Cover art © 2000 by Richard James Cook, from the book *Angel of Light*

ISBN-10:1936665190
ISBN 13: 978-1-936665-19-8

Table of Contents

Loss and Healing

When someone close to you dies, the impact is life changing. The grief process can be very difficult, and it is important to find support and guidance. "Being strong" or "toughing it out" is not the answer. Grief cannot be denied. Religion does not eliminate the need to grieve. "Blessed are they that mourn, for they shall be comforted," said Jesus, suggesting that God can indeed comfort us if we allow ourselves to work through the pain.

In the midst of grief, it's often hard to know what you need. One thing that can help is to realize that your spirit has suffered a very serious wound. When your body suffers a serious wound it must be attended to, and emotional wounds are just as real. You need rest, nourishing food, love and support. You need to remove as many other stresses from your life as possible. Sometimes you'll require company, sometimes solitude—sometimes sleep, sometimes movement and activity. Sometimes you'll need help from family, friends, or professionals. Sometimes you'll do better on your own.

Do not doubt that healing can and will happen. In the case of a serious physical wound, you may need the help of a doctor. A doctor cannot actually heal you, but can stitch the wound or provide other help that will allow the healing to take place. It is God's deep and tender love that brings about the actual mending.

It is the same with a serious emotional wound. You may need help from others to allow the healing to take place. And it will. Here again, God will make it happen.

Let others help you with things that overwhelm you. Seek out support groups or books that can help you make sense of your emotions. Pay attention, be honest with yourself, and you will often sense what you need. Trust these feelings, and act on them. Do what you need to, to provide conditions for healing.

Wait on the Lord; be of good courage
and He shall strengthen your heart.

Psalm 27:14

Introduction to Journal Pages

It is you who will write most of this book.

Keeping a journal is recommended by grief experts as one tool you can use in working your way through grief. The anguish of coming to terms with the absence of someone who has died can be debilitating and confusing. You might not even know what you need or where to turn. Writing about your thoughts and feelings can help to clarify your needs.

A journal is a place where your heart can speak in privacy and freedom. It is a place where it is safe to be completely honest about what you are thinking and how you are feeling. It can uncover thoughts and emotions you may be scarcely aware of. Putting issues on paper, both negative and positive, can provide more insight into both your pain and your progress and help guide you toward healing. It may even help to free you from troubling thoughts that seem to be stuck on "replay" in your mind.

Some use writing as a place to speak with their loved one or to God. These letters can express gratitude and love or acknowledge anger, regrets and fears. Recording these can be valuable in sorting out perplexing or conflicting patterns.

Another benefit of keeping a journal is that it provides a chance to observe ups and downs over a period of time. Entries of despair and entries of peace may only be pages apart. When feeling desperate, you may think you'll never feel peaceful again. When feeling peaceful, you may think the desperation is over. Writing and rereading can help clarify the undulating nature of grief and help you to find balance.

This is your journal. Freely use it in ways that are best for you. The hope and prayer is that it will help you along your path. Begin when you are ready.

Date

*Treat yourself with patience
and understanding.*

Tell others what you need.

Date

Isn't it amazing that the world around
you goes on as before?

"Death cancels everything but truth."
Anonymous

> Don't expect recovery to be a straight line.
> It is a fluctuating line with both peaks
> and valleys.

Take one day at a time.

Supressed feelings can't be healed.

Find a place where you can shout or cry.

Date

Sleeping too much or sleeping too little . . .
eating too much or eating too little . . .
all can be symptoms of grief.

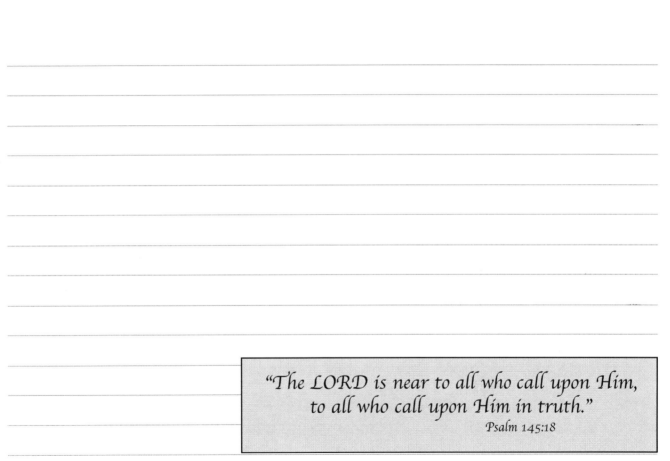

"The LORD is near to all who call upon Him,
to all who call upon Him in truth."

Psalm 145:18

Look for physical symptoms
of emotional wounds.

> Anger is often fear or sadness
> in disguise.

Date

Emotional wounds and physical wounds
need time and attention in order to heal.

"Thus says the LORD . . .
I have heard your prayer, I have seen your
tears; surely I will heal you."
2 Kings 20:5

Date

Forgetting things, losing things, having difficulty making decisions are all typical symptoms of grief.

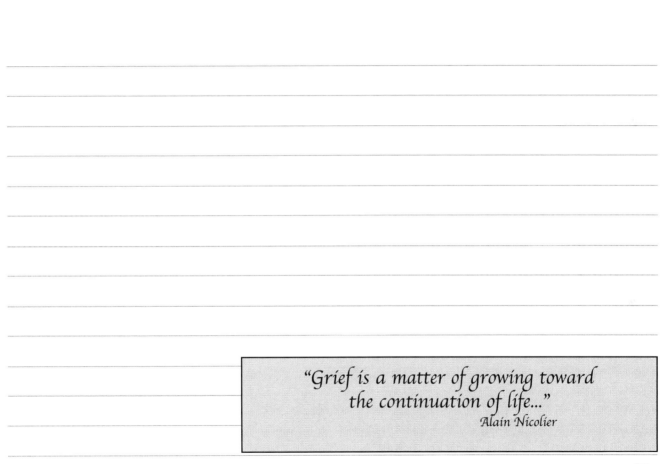

"Grief is a matter of growing toward
the continuation of life..."
Alain Nicolier

> Forgive those who do not understand
> and find those who do.

> "The absence of God from a person is no more possible than the absence of the sun from the earth."
>
> Emanuel Swedenborg

> *Those things you wish you had said or done can still be said and done in other ways.*

> *Beware of false guilt. Usually regret is more appropriate than guilt.*

Write to this person you miss so much and tell them the truth about your love and pain. Write a reply from what you imagine his/her perspective to be.

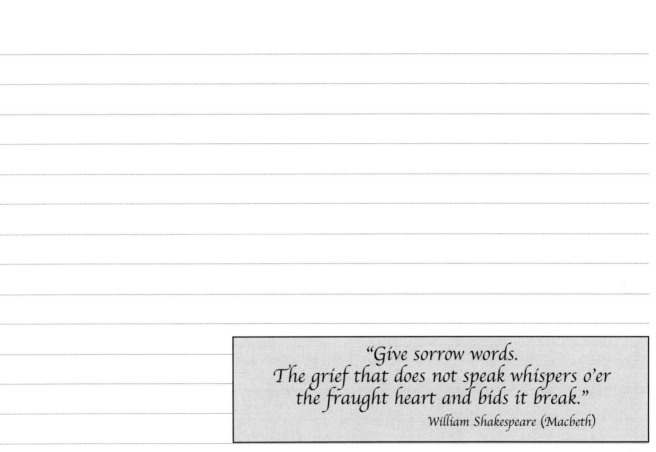

"Give sorrow words.
The grief that does not speak whispers o'er
the fraught heart and bids it break."

William Shakespeare (Macbeth)

Grieving is exhausting. Take care of yourself.

"The LORD my God
will enlighten my darkness."
Psalm 18:28

Grief is an emotion, not a disease.
Beware of drugs that may delay recovery.

Be willing to ask for help.

Sometimes nothing makes sense, because
perspective on everything changes when you
experience something of this magnitude.

Sometimes a loss activates emotions
from previous losses.

Date

Numbness is common in grief and serves
a purpose. It gives you rest.

> "Come unto Me, all you who labor and are
> burdened, and I will give you rest."
> Matthew 11:28

Don't be hurt by those who say
the wrong thing. They are struggling
and don't know what to say.

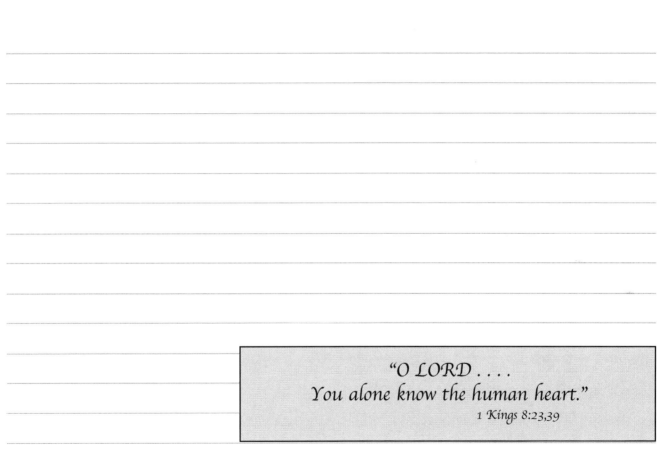

"O LORD . . . .
You alone know the human heart."
1 Kings 8:23,39

To avoid grieving is to complicate grieving.

> "Cast your burdens upon the LORD
> and He shall sustain you."
> Psalm 55:22

Date

God understands
and grieves with you.

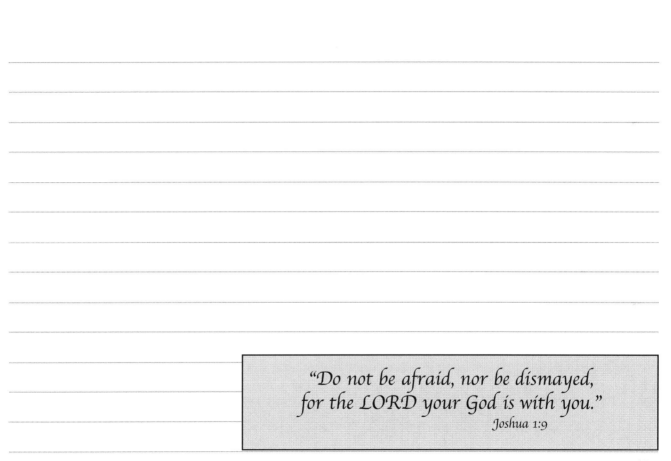

"Do not be afraid, nor be dismayed,
for the LORD your God is with you."

Joshua 1:9

Grief visits all of us. Celebrities grieve, counselors grieve, bishops grieve and even Jesus wept.

"Sorrow makes us all children again."
Ralph Waldo Emerson

Date

When alone you may crave company.
In company you may crave solitude.

Forgive yourself for
your "craziness."

Date

Try to be aware of and patient with those
close to you. They are suffering their own
grief in their own way.

> "Any child old enough to love is old
> enough to mourn . . ."
> Alan Wolfelt

Date

Within you lies the power to heal.

"Beyond our despair lies our deliverance."
Brant M. Kirkland

Date _____

Grief is a physical, social, emotional,
and spiritual experience.

Attend to what you need on all levels.

Date _____

You grieve because
you love.

"Each dear friend that I have 'lost'
is a link between this world and the next."
Helen Keller

Tears are a gift that serve both physical and emotional needs.

"Take this sorrow to thy heart, and make it a part of thee, and it shall nourish thee till thou art strong again."

Henry Wadsworth Longfellow

God never sleeps. Talk to God now.

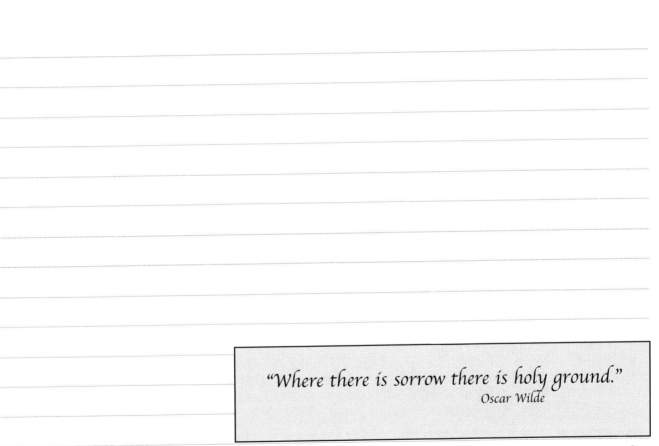

"Where there is sorrow there is holy ground."
Oscar Wilde

Date

Every spring season is evidence of
the continuation of life.

> *"Every single moment of a person's life, both of the understanding and of the will, is a new beginning."*
> Emanuel Swedenborg

Date

Special days can be less difficult than you
imagine and even uplifting. Make plans for
them rather than dreading or enduring them.

Create a place or a ritual you can visit.

Date

Grief is both universal and very personal.
Many can understand,
but no one knows "just how you feel."

> "... without death, there would be no awareness of life ..."
> Charles A. Lindbergh

Time moves slowly—the painful hours
and days can seem endless. Surprisingly
the years go quickly.

"Life is the childhood of our immortality."
Johann Wolfgang von Goethe

Don't ever expect to return to "normal." You are forever changed but you will eventually find that you are more than you were, not less.

"Grief drives men into habits of serious reflection,
sharpens the understanding and softens the heart."
John Adams

Date ....

We are all spiritual beings and dwell
together in love. There is no separation
or distance on that plane.

> "Great are they who see that the spiritual is stronger than any material force."
> Ralph Waldo Emerson

> Notice something beautiful today—
> especially if nothing has seemed beautiful
> for a long time.

> "Sadness flies on the wings of the morning,
> and out of the heart of darkness comes light."
>
> Jean Giraudoux

Date _____

Don't dwell on unpleasant circumstances
that surrounded your loved one's death.
Right now your loved one is alive and happy,
and doesn't want you to suffer.

> "Death—the last sleep?
> No, it is the final awakening."
> Walter Scott

Date ....

There will come a time when gratitude for
knowing and loving this person may replace the
pain of your loss.

"Before we can hear God speaking...
our hearts must be prepared to listen."
Ken Gire

Date

> You are changed because of this death, just as you were changed when this person came into your life.

Relationships do not end with death.

You may find your grief triggered at unexpected times in unexpected places. Some triggers are predictable and some are unexplainable.

"Grief teaches the steadiest minds to waver."

Antigone

Date ....

....

....

....

....

....

....

....

....

> *The body of your loved one is gone.*
> *The spirit of that person still lives*
> *and is a permanent part of you.*

"It is not the body, but thought together with affection that make a person."
Emanuel Swedenborg

Date

There is no absolute time table for grieving.
It takes longer than expected.

Save this journal.
Reading it at intervals may be helpful.

The promise of eternity is consolation
for the shortness of earthly life.

> "We are unable in this world to understand the peace of heaven, because human words are inadequate."
>
> Emanuel Swedenborg

Date

Notice the fear of letting go of your grief.
This may feel like betrayal, but it is not.

> *"The ocean has its ebbings—and so has grief."*
> Thomas Campbell

Date _____

You can't hold them in your arms, but you can hold them in your heart. And you'll hold them in your arms again one day.

Love is indestructable.

Life After Death

According to the Gallup Poll, a large majority of Americans believe that death is not the end of life. Many of those who have lost a loved one believe that though the body died the unique personality, loves and qualities of the person continue to live in a new body in a more perfect world.

Helen Keller speaks of her certainty that after "death" she would not only continue to live but would live in a body free of the disabilities she endured while in this world. She writes: "I believe that when the eyes within my physical eyes open upon the world to come, I will be consciously living in the country of my heart."

This feeling of being in the "country of my heart" or feeling that they were "home" is often described by those who have had Near Death Experiences (NDEs). First Raymond Moody then Kenneth Ring, Archie Matson and others describe the joy and peace experienced by those who "died" but were brought back to life. To most of them life after death is now a certainty.

Jacquelyn Oliveira speaks of "those physically near us here on earth, and those spiritually near us to eternity" in her book called *The Case For Life Beyond Death*.

There are countless other books addressing the conviction that life in this world is only the beginning. Emanuel Swedenborg offers more details about the life of heaven.

"We do not die—we simply pass from one world into the next."
Emanuel Swedenborg, *Heaven and Hell 445*

According to Swedenborg, whatever the circumstances of the death you mourn, this person is now experiencing great peace and excitement exploring the wonders of the next life.

"We are not human beings because of our bodies but because of our spirits."
Emanuel Swedenborg, *Heaven and Hell* 445

The body of your loved one is gone but the spirit of that person continues to dwell with you and cannot be taken from you.

"Life in time is but a fleeting shadow compared with never ending enjoyment and bliss of life in eternity."
Emanuel Swedenborg, *Divine Providence* 73

There is no earthly time for those in the next life so they can look forward to a reunion with you without anguish or impatience. From this side it is not that easy, but as you discover ways you are still joined in love and in common goals, you may also find peace.

> *"And now, LORD, what do I wait for?*
> *My hope is in You."*
> Psalm 39:7

Recommended Reading About Grief

ON DEATH AND DYING and ON CHILDREN AND DEATH, by Elisabeth Kubler-Ross
Two of many books by Elisabeth Kubler-Ross

THE GRIEF RECOVERY HANDBOOK, by John W. James and Russel Friedman
"Moving beyond death, divorce, and other losses."
". . . unresolved grief is the major underlying issue in most people's lives."

WHEN BAD THINGS HAPPEN TO GOOD PEOPLE, by Harold S. Kushner.
"(There are) people around you, and God beside you, and strength within you to help you survive."

A JOURNEY THROUGH GRIEF, by Alla Renee Bozarth
"Pace yourself lovingly and remember – this pain won't last forever."

HEALING YOUR GRIEVING HEART, by Alan D. Wolfelt
"Compassionate advice and simple activities to help you through your loss."

THE MOURNING HANDBOOK, by Helen Fitzgerald
"Practical and compassionate advice on coping with all aspects of death and dying."

LIVING WHEN A LOVED ONE HAS DIED, by Earl A. Grollman
"Your recovering is not an act of disloyalty to the one who has died."

About Life After Death

HEAVEN AND HELL, by Emanuel Swedenborg
"We do not die, we simply pass from one world into another."

A BOOK ABOUT DYING: PREPARING FOR ETERNAL LIFE, by Robert Kirven
"The end of our body's life is not the end of our life."

WINDOW TO ETERNITY, by Bruce Henderson
"...Your spiritual life is not something that begins when you die. It starts the moment you are born..."

TUNNEL TO ETERNITY: BEYOND NEAR DEATH, by Leon S. Rhodes
".. Increasingly we are able to raise our thoughts above this limited physical world."

HELLO FROM HEAVEN, by Bill Guggenheim and Judy Guggenheim
"Over and over, ADCs [After Death Communications] confirm that there is a life after death and our deceased loved ones continue to exist."

LIFE AFTER LIFE, by Raymond Moody
"Actual case histories that reveal there is life after death."

ON LIFE AFTER DEATH, by Elisabeth Kubler-Ross
"Our physical body is only the shell that encloses our immortal self."

A DOVE AT THE WINDOW: LIVING DREAMS AND SPIRITUAL EXPERIENCES, by Vera P. Glenn
"There is another world beyond the material one. It is peopled with human beings from the earth and wisely governed by a loving God."

Also by Donnette Alfelt:
COMFORT AND HOPE FOR WIDOWS AND WIDOWERS
The death of your spouse is not the end of your relationship.

We want this journal to be of help and comfort, and we
welcome your feedback. Contact us through our website
at www.fountainpublishing.com, or write to
Fountain Publishing. P.O. Box 80011, Rochester MI 48308

Made in the USA
Columbia, SC
01 July 2022

62530853R00062